Bread

The Taunton Press

ACADEMIA BARILLA
AMBASSADOR OF ITALIAN GASTRONOMY
THROUGHOUT THE WORLD

Academia Barilla is a global movement toward the protection, development and promotion of authentic regional Italian culture and cuisine.
With the concept of Food as Culture at our core, Academia Barilla offers a 360° view of Italy. Our comprehensive approach includes:

- a state-of-the-art culinary center in Parma, Italy;
- gourmet travel programs and hands-on cooking classes;
- the world's largest Italian gastronomic library and historic menu collection;
- a portfolio of premium artisan food products;
- global culinary certification programs;
- custom corporate services and training;
- team building activities;
- and a vast assortment of Italian cookbooks.

Thank you and we look forward to welcoming you in Italy soon!

CONTENTS

EDITED BY
ACADEMIA BARILLA

PHOTOGRAPHS
ALBERTO ROSSI

RECIPES BY
GIOVANNI GANDINO
CHEF MARIO GRAZIA

TEXT BY
MARIAGRAZIA VILLA

ACADEMIA BARILLA EDITORIAL COORDINATION
CHATO MORANDI
ILARIA ROSSI
REBECCA PICKRELL

GRAPHIC DESIGN
PAOLA PIACCO

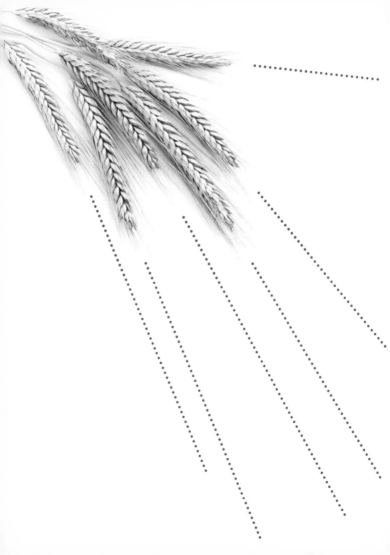

THE SIMPLE FLAVORS GIVE THE SAME
PLEASURE AS THE MOST REFINED. WATER AND
A PIECE OF BREAD GIVE GREATEST PLEASURE
TO SOMEONE WHO IS IN WANT OF THEM.

EPICURUS, *LETTER TO MENOECEUS,*
ALSO CALLED *THE LETTER ON HAPPINESS,*
3RD CENTURY B.C.

BREAD

There is nothing easier than kneading together flour, water, yeast and salt. There's nothing more elementary than setting the dough aside to rise until it increases in volume. And nothing could be more simple than using your hands to shape the forms to bake in the oven. Making bread is a ritual, with a formula of steps that lead, one after the other, to the desired goal. There's no need for beginners' anxiety or a rigid pursuit of perfection. When baking bread, it is important to have a lighthearted, positive attitude—to experiment, to have fun and be willing to try again. You just need to follow some basic rules.

Bread has a good number of crispy relatives, like breadsticks and crackers—so tantalizing they can be enjoyed any time of the day. A more modern version of bread, they have a well-established tradition in Italy, not least because they so easily digested. (Cracker dough has less moisture content than bread, and makes for easier digestion.)

In this volume, you'll find 40 recipes for bread, breadsticks and crackers selected by Academia Barilla, the international center dedicated to the preservation and promotion of Italian gastronomy. The recipes include everyday breads, like Milk Rolls; specialties, like Bread Triangles with Radicchio di Treviso; local varieties, like Taralli, from

Puglia; and fanciful treats, like Peanut Croissants. Italy is a Land of Bread, as evidenced by the many bread-related sayings and proverbs that abound in the national language. And, after all, it is a food we cannot get by without. We would not dream of a meal, even the most frugal, that is not accompanied by bread. Sometimes, it is a course in itself. It is said that the great sculptor Michelangelo ate only bread while he worked. In its sublime simplicity, bread has embodied life, peace and welcoming since ancient times, and it was considered sacred long before the advent of Christianity. It has been a constant in the long history of the Italian people, particularly after the Renaissance when—thanks to the revolution of yeast, possibly to the credit of Maria de' Medici's cooks—it gained in softness.

In Italy, soft-wheat, or "00" flour is used, but is not as readily available in the U.S. So for this book we have substituted all-purpose flour or cake flour in the recipes. However, if you have access to Italian "00" flour (which is available online and in some Italian specialty markets), give it a try.

There are some 250 types of local breads produced in the *Bel Paese*, the "beautiful country," as Italians call their home, some of which are historical and have remained unchanged for centuries. Here is a taste!

WALNUT CANNOLI

Preparation time: 10 minutes   Rising time: 1 hour 10 minutes
Cooking time: 15 minutes   Difficulty: easy

10 SERVINGS

8 cups (1 kg) **all-purpose flour** *or cake flour, plus more as needed*
2 1/3 cups (550 ml) **warm water** *(105°–115°F/41°–46°C)*
3 1/2 oz. (100 g) **walnuts**, *coarsely ground*
3 tbsp. (40 g) **unsalted butter**, *softened*
1 tbsp. plus 3/4 tsp. (10 g) **active dry yeast**
1 tbsp. plus 1 tsp. (25 g) **salt**

Put the flour on a clean work surface and make a well in the center. Add the walnuts. Dissolve the yeast in the water and pour the yeast mixture into the well. Gradually start incorporating the yeast mixture into the flour mixture until a loose dough starts to form, then add the butter and salt. Knead until the dough is smooth and elastic.

Heat the oven to 350°F (175°C). Cover the dough with a sheet of plastic wrap, let it rest for about 10 minutes, then roll it out to a thickness of about 3/4 inch (2 cm). Cut out strips about 2 1/3 inch (6 cm) wide and roll them up to make the cannoli. Arrange the cannoli, floured and well spaced, in a baking pan lined with parchment paper. Let the dough rise in a warm place, covered with a sheet of plastic wrap, until it has doubled in size, about 1 hour. Bake for about 15 minutes, or until golden brown.

CIABATTA LOAF

Preparation time: 10 minutes   Rising time: 1 hour 10 minutes
Cooking time: 25 minutes   Difficulty: easy

10 SERVINGS

4 cups (500 g) **all-purpose flour or cake flour**, *plus more as needed*
4 1/4 cups (500 g) **whole-wheat flour**, *plus more as needed*
3 1/4 cups (750 ml) **warm water** *(105°–115°F/41°–46°C)*
2 tbsp. plus 2 tsp. (40 ml) **extra-virgin olive oil**
1 tbsp. plus 3/4 tsp. (10 g) **active dry yeast**
1 tbsp. plus 1 tsp. (25 g) **salt**

Mix the two types of flour in a large bowl and make a well in the mixture.
Dissolve the yeast in the water and pour the yeast mixture into the well.
Gradually start incorporating the yeast mixture into the flour mixture until a loose
dough starts to form, then add the oil and salt. (The dough will be soft and
sticky.) Knead until the dough is smooth and soft. (Do not add flour, even though
the dough seems to be extremely soft.)
Heat the oven to 340°F (170°C). Sprinkle flour on the dough and let it rest,
covered with a sheet of plastic wrap, for about 10 minutes. Then cut up the
dough into pieces about 5 to 7 ounces (150–200 g), flattening each one lightly
with your fingers into the shape of a *ciabatta* (Italian for "slipper"). Sprinkle
generously with whole-wheat flour to give the bread its typical rustic color and
taste when cooked, and arrange the dough in a baking pan lined with
parchment paper. Let the dough rise in a warm place, covered with a sheet of
plastic wrap, until it has doubled in size, about 1 hour. Bake for about 25
minutes, or until golden brown.

PEANUT CROISSANTS

Preparation time: 10 minutes   Rising time: 1 hour 10 minutes
Cooking time: 20 minutes   Difficulty: easy

10 SERVINGS

8 cups (1 kg) **all-purpose flour or cake flour**, *plus more as needed*
2 1/3 cups (550 ml) **warm water** *(105°–115°F/41°–46°C)*
1 tbsp. plus 3/4 tsp. (10 g) **active dry yeast**
12 1/3 oz. (350 g) **peanuts**
1/4 stick (30 g) **unsalted butter**, *softened*
1 tbsp. plus 1 tsp. (25 g) **salt**

Toast, peel, then coarsely grind the peanuts. Put the flour on a clean work surface and make a well in the center. Add the peanuts. Dissolve the yeast in the water and pour the yeast mixture into the well. Gradually start incorporating the yeast mixture into the flour mixture until a loose dough starts to form, then add the butter and salt. Knead until the dough is smooth and elastic.

Heat the oven to 350°F (175°C). Cover the dough with a sheet of plastic wrap and let it rest for about 10 minutes. Using a rolling pin, roll the dough to a thickness of about 3/4 inch (2 cm). Cut out triangles and roll them up into croissants. Arrange the pieces, floured and well spaced, in a baking pan lined with parchment paper. Let the dough rise in a warm place, covered with a sheet of plastic wrap, until it has doubled in size, about 1 hour. Bake for about 20 minutes, or until golden brown.

SOYBEAN LOAF

Preparation time: 10 minutes   Rising time: 1 hour 10 minutes
Cooking time: 20 minutes   Difficulty: easy

10 SERVINGS

8 cups (1 kg) **all-purpose flour or cake flour**, *plus more as needed*
2 1/8 cups (500 ml) **warm water** *(105°–115°F/41°–46°C)*
1 tbsp. plus 3/4 tsp. (10 g) **active dry yeast**
8 4/5 oz. (250 g) **soybeans**, *boiled*
3 tbsp. (40 g) **unsalted butter**, *softened*
1 tbsp. plus 1 tsp. (25 g) **salt**

Put the flour on a clean work surface and make a well in the center. Dissolve the
yeast in the water and pour the yeast mixture into the well. Gradually start
incorporating the yeast mixture into the flour until a loose dough starts to form,
then add the butter, the soybeans and the salt. Knead until the dough is smooth
and elastic.
Heat the oven to 350°F (175°C). Cover the dough with a sheet of plastic wrap
and let it rest for about 10 minutes; then divide it into 2-ounce (60 g) pieces and
roll them into ropes about 10 inches (25 cm) long. Arrange the ropes, floured
and well spaced, in a baking pan lined with parchment paper. Let the dough rise
in a warm place, covered with a sheet of plastic wrap, until it has doubled in size,
about 1 hour. Make deep incisions along the lengths of the ropes and bake
them for about 20 minutes, or until golden brown.

POTATO LOAF

Preparation time: 1 hour   Rising time: 1 hour 10 minutes
Cooking time: 20 minutes   Difficulty: easy

10 SERVINGS

8 cups (1 kg) **all-purpose flour or cake flour**, *plus more as needed*
2 1/3 cups (550 ml) **warm water** *(105°–115°F/41°–46°C)*
1 tbsp. plus 3/4 tsp. (10 g) **active dry yeast**
14 oz. (400 g) **potatoes**
3 tbsp. (40 g) **unsalted butter**, *softened*
1 tbsp. plus 1 tsp. (25 g) **salt**

Clean and wash the potatoes and boil them in a pot of salted water. Drain, peel
and dice them into 1/3-inch (1-cm) cubes. Put the flour on a clean work surface
and make a well in the center. Dissolve the yeast in the water and pour the yeast
mixture into the well. Gradually start incorporating the yeast mixture into the
flour until a loose dough starts to form, then add the butter and the potatoes.
Lastly, add the salt and continue to knead until the dough is smooth and elastic.
Heat the oven to 350°F (175°C). Cover the dough with a sheet of plastic wrap
and let it rest for about 10 minutes; then divide it into pieces, each weighing
about 2 ounces (60 g). Roll them into ropes and bend each one into
the shape of a horseshoe.
Arrange the u-shaped loaves, floured and well spaced, in a baking pan lined
with parchment paper. Let the dough rise in a warm place, covered with a sheet
of plastic wrap, until it has doubled in size, about 1 hour. Make deep incisions
around the tops of the horseshoes and bake them for about 20 minutes,
or until golden brown.

OAT LOAVES

Preparation time: 10 minutes   Rising time: 1 hour 10 minutes
Cooking time: 15 minutes   Difficulty: easy

10 SERVINGS

4 3/4 cups (600 g) **all-purpose flour or cake flour***, plus more as needed*
3 1/3 cups (400 g) **whole-wheat flour**
2 1/2 cups (600 ml) **warm water** *(105°–115°F/41°–46°C)*
3 tbsp. (40 g) **unsalted butter***, softened*
4 1/2 tsp. (12 g) **active dry yeast**
1 tbsp. plus 1 tsp. (25 g) **salt**
Oat flakes*, as needed*

Combine the two types of flour. Put the flours on a clean work surface and make a well in the center. Put the flour on a clean work surface and make a well in the center. Dissolve the yeast in the water and pour the yeast mixture into the well. Gradually start incorporating the yeast mixture into the flour mixture until a loose dough starts to form, then add the butter and a few oat flakes. Lastly, add the salt and continue to knead until the dough is smooth and elastic.

Heat the oven to 350°F (175°C). Cover the dough with a sheet of plastic wrap and let it rest for about 10 minutes; then form small loaves, each weighing about 3 1/2 ounces (100 g). Moisten the surface with a little room-temperature water and sprinkle with oat flakes. Arrange the loaves, well spaced, in a baking pan lined with parchment paper. Let the dough rise in a warm place, covered with a sheet of plastic wrap, until it has doubled in size, about 1 hour. Bake for about 15 minutes, or until golden brown.

MINT TWISTS

Preparation time: 15 minutes   Rising time: 1 hour 10 minutes
Cooking time: 15 minutes   Difficulty: easy

10 SERVINGS

*8 cups (1 kg) **all-purpose flour or cake flour**, plus more as needed*
*About 30 **fresh mint leaves**, or about 1/8 cup (10 g) **dried mint***
*2 1/2 cups (600 ml) **warm water** (105°–115°F/41°–46°C)*
*1 tbsp. plus 3/4 tsp. (10 g) **active dry yeast***
*1/2 stick (50 g) **unsalted butter**, softened*
*1 tbsp. (20 g) **salt***

If you are using fresh mint, rinse and dry the leaves. Tear the leaves into small
pieces, add them to the butter and mix them together to make a spreadable
cream. If you are using dried mint, add it directly to the flour. Put the flour on a
clean work surface and make a well in the center. Dissolve the yeast in the water
and pour the yeast mixture into the well. Gradually start incorporating the yeast
mixture into the flour mixture until a loose dough starts to form, then add the
butter and salt. Knead until the dough is smooth and elastic.
Heat the oven to 360°F (180°C). Cover the dough with a sheet of plastic wrap
and let it rest for about 10 minutes; then break it into pieces about 1 3/4 ounces
(50 g) each and roll them into ropes about 8 inches (20 cm) long. Tie them into
knots. Arrange them, floured and well spaced, in a baking pan lined with
parchment paper. Let the dough rise in a warm place, covered with a sheet of
plastic wrap, until it has doubled in size, about 1 hour. Bake for about 15
minutes, or until golden brown.

BRIOCHES WITH DATES

Preparation time: 20 minutes   Rising time: 1 hour 10 minutes
Cooking time: 15 minutes   Difficulty: medium

10 SERVINGS

8 cups (1 kg) **all-purpose flour or cake flour**, *plus more as needed*
1/2 cup (100 g) **sugar**
1/2 cup (100 ml) **warm milk**
About 20 **dates**, *cut into strips*
8 **eggs**, *room temperature*
2 tbsp. (16 g) **active dry yeast**
1/2 stick (50 g) **unsalted butter**, *softened*
Salt *to taste*

Put the flour on a clean work surface and make a well in the center. Dissolve the
yeast in the milk and the sugar and pour the yeast mixture into the well.
Gradually start incorporating the yeast mixture into the flour mixture until a loose
dough starts to form, then add the eggs, one at a time. Add the butter, the
dates and, lastly, the salt. Knead until the dough is smooth and elastic.
Heat the oven to 325°F (160°C). Cover the dough with a sheet of plastic wrap
and let it rest for about 10 minutes; then divide it into pieces, each weighing
about 1 3/4 ounces (50 g). Place the brioches, floured and well spaced (bear in
mind that brioche dough increases in size considerably during cooking), in a
baking pan lined with parchment paper. Let the dough rise in a warm place,
covered with a sheet of plastic wrap, until it has doubled in size, about 1 hour.
Bake for about 15 minutes, or until golden brown.

CARASAU FLATBREAD

Preparation time: 30 minutes   Rising time: 3 hours 30 minutes
Cooking time: 2 minutes   Difficulty: high

4 SERVINGS

3 cups (350 g) **semolina flour**, *plus more as needed*
3/4 cup (175 ml) **warm water** *(105°–115°F/41°–46°C)*

Put the flour on a clean work surface and make a well in the center. Pour the water into the well. Gradually knead the flour and water together to obtain a rather dense dough. Let it rest in a warm place, covered with a sheet of plastic wrap, for at least 30 minutes.

Divide the dough into pieces of approximately 3 1/2 ounces (100 grams) each, and form them into balls. Roll out the dough balls into rounds with a thickness of about 1/25 inch (1 mm). Stack the dough rounds, placing lightly floured napkins between them, and let them rest for about 3 hours.

Bake the rounds in the oven (preferably a pizza oven, directly on the hearth, at 660°F/350°C, or in a traditional oven at 500°F/260°C, using a preheated baking stone or parchment-lined sheet tray) until they inflate like balloons, after about 45 to 60 seconds.

Using a sharp knife, cut the puffed rounds open along their circumference to obtain two separate rounds. Return these cooked rounds to the oven for another 1 to 2 minutes, a second baking (a process called *carasare* in the Sardinian language), which makes them dry and crunchy.

SPINACH LOAF

Preparation time: 30 minutes   Rising time: 1 hour 10 minutes
Cooking time: 1 hour   Difficulty: easy

10 SERVINGS

8 cups (1 kg) **all-purpose flour or cake flour**, *plus more as needed*
2 1/8 cups (500 ml) **warm water** *(105°–115°F/41°–46°C)*
1 lb. (200 g) **fresh spinach**
1/2 tsp. (1 g) **ground nutmeg**
Pinch of **pepper**
1 tbsp. plus 3/4 tsp. (10 g) **active dry yeast**
1/2 stick (50 g) **unsalted butter**, *softened*
1 tbsp. plus 1 tsp. (25 g) **salt**
Oil, for pan

Prepare the spinach purée: Remove the stalks and thoroughly wash the spinach.
Cook it in a pot of boiling water, then drain and purée it in a food processor.
Put the flour on a clean work surface and make a well in the center. Add the
spinach purée, pepper and nutmeg. Dissolve the yeast in the water and pour the
yeast mixture into the well. Gradually start incorporating the yeast mixture into
the flour mixture until a loose dough starts to form, then add the butter and salt.
Knead until the dough is smooth and elastic.
Heat the oven to 425°F (220°C). Let the dough rest, covered with a sheet of
plastic wrap, for about 10 minutes; then place it in a lidded loaf pan (see photo
of the Pullman loaf pan) that is lightly oiled—filling it no more than halfway.
Close the lid, but leave a small opening to check the dough rising, which will
take about 1 hour. When the dough rises to the top of pan, close it completely
and bake for about 40 minutes. Remove the pan from the oven and the bread
from the pan, then put the bread back in the oven to finish baking for at least 20
minutes, or until a toothpick inserted in the bread comes out clean.

SUN-DRIED TOMATO ROLLS

Preparation time: 10 minutes   Rising time: 1 hour 10 minutes
Cooking time: 20 minutes   Difficulty: easy

10 SERVINGS

8 cups (1 kg) **all-purpose flour or cake flour**, plus more as needed
2 1/8 cups (500 ml) **warm water** (105°–115°F/41°–46°C)
1 tbsp. plus 3/4 tsp. (10 g) **active dry yeast**
3 1/2 oz. (100 g) **sun-dried tomatoes in oil**
2 tbsp. (30 ml) **oil**
1 tbsp. plus 1 tsp. (25 g) **salt**

Drain the oil from the sun-dried tomatoes and julienne them. Put the flour on a
clean work surface and make a well in the center. Dissolve the yeast in the water
and pour the yeast mixture into the well. Gradually start incorporating the yeast
mixture into the flour until a loose dough starts to form, then add the oil
and the sun-dried tomatoes. Lastly, add the salt and continue to knead until
the dough is smooth and elastic.

Heat the oven to 350°F (175°C). Cover the dough with a sheet of plastic wrap
and let it rest for about 10 minutes; then divide it into pieces, each weighing
about 1 3/4 ounces (50 g). Form rolls in the shape of ripe tomatoes. Arrange the
rolls, floured and well spaced, in a baking pan lined with parchment. Let the
dough rise in a warm place, covered with a sheet of plastic wrap, until it has
doubled in size, about 1 hour. Bake for about 20 minutes, or until golden brown.
Garnish with tomato vines, if desired.

MIXED-SEED ROLLS

Preparation time: 10 minutes   Rising time: 1 hour 10 minutes
Cooking time: 12 minutes   Difficulty: easy

10 SERVINGS

8 cups (1 kg) **all-purpose flour or cake flour**, *plus more as needed*
2 1/8 cups (500 ml) **warm milk**
Poppy seeds *and/or* **cumin seeds**, *and/or* **sunflower seeds**,
and/or **sesame seeds** *(to decorate)*
3 tbsp. (40 g) **unsalted butter**, *softened*
1 tbsp. plus 3/4 tsp. (10 g) **active dry yeast**
1 tbsp. plus 1 tsp. (25 g) **salt**

Put the flour on a clean work surface and make a well in the center. Dissolve the
yeast in the water and pour the yeast mixture into the well. Gradually start
incorporating the yeast mixture into the flour until a loose dough starts to form,
then add the butter and the salt. Knead until the dough is smooth and elastic.
Heat the oven to 350°F (175°C). Cover the dough with a sheet of plastic wrap
and let it rest for about 10 minutes; then form small rolls, each weighing about 1
ounce (30 g). Moisten the surface of the rolls with a little room-temperature
water and coat with seeds of your choice. Arrange the rolls, well spaced, in a
baking pan lined with parchment paper. Let the dough rise in a warm place,
covered with a sheet of plastic wrap, until it has doubled in size, about 1 hour.
Bake for about 12 minutes, or until golden brown.

BASIL ROLLS

Preparation time: 10 minutes   Rising time: 1 hour 10 minutes
Cooking time: 15 minutes   Difficulty: easy

10 SERVINGS

8 cups (1 kg) **all-purpose flour or cake flour**, *plus more as needed*
25 **fresh basil leaves**, *torn finely*
2 1/2 cups (600 ml) **warm water** *(105°–115°F/41°–46°C)*
1 tbsp. plus 3/4 tsp. (10 g) **active dry yeast**
1/2 stick (50 g) **unsalted butter**, *softened*
1 tbsp. (20 g) **salt**

Mix the basil leaves into the flour. Put the flour on a clean work surface and make a well in the center. Dissolve the yeast in the water and pour the yeast mixture into the well. Gradually start incorporating the yeast mixture into the flour mixture until a loose dough starts to form, then add the butter and the salt. Knead until the dough is smooth and elastic.

Heat the oven to 360°F (180°C). Cover the dough with a sheet of plastic wrap and let it rest for about 10 minutes; then form it into small balls, each weighing about 1 3/4 ounces (50 g). Arrange them, floured and well spaced, in a baking pan lined with parchment paper. Let the dough rise in a warm place, covered with a sheet of plastic wrap, until it has doubled in size, about 1 hour. Bake for about 15 minutes, or until golden brown.

SUNFLOWER-SEED ROLLS

Preparation time: 10 minutes   Rising time: 1 hour 10 minutes
Cooking time: 12 minutes   Difficulty: easy

10 SERVINGS

8 cups (1 kg) **all-purpose flour or cake flour,** *plus more as needed*
2 1/8 cups (500 ml) **warm water** *(105°–115°F/41°–46°C)*
Sunflower seeds, *as needed*
3 tbsp. (40 g) **unsalted butter,** *softened*
1 tbsp. plus 3/4 tsp. (10 g) **active dry yeast**
1 tbsp. plus 1 tsp. (25 g) **salt**

Put the flour on a clean work surface and make a well in the center. Dissolve the
yeast in the water and pour the yeast mixture into the well. Gradually start
incorporating the yeast mixture into the flour until a loose dough starts to form,
then add the butter, some sunflower seeds and the salt. Knead until
the dough is smooth and elastic.
Heat the oven to 350°F (175°C). Cover the dough with a sheet of plastic wrap
and let it rest for about 10 minutes; then form small rolls, each weighing about
1 3/4 ounces (50 g). Moisten the surface of the rolls with a little
room-temperature water and sprinkle with sunflower seeds. Arrange the rolls,
floured and well spaced, in a baking pan lined with parchment paper. Let the
dough rise in a warm place, covered with a sheet of plastic wrap, until it has
doubled in size, about 1 hour. Bake for about 12 minutes, or until golden brown.

MILK ROLLS

Preparation time: 10 minutes Rising time: 1 hour 10 minutes
Cooking time: 20 minutes Difficulty: easy

10 SERVINGS

8 cups (1 kg) **all-purpose flour or cake flour**, *plus more as needed*
2 3/4 cups (650 ml) **warm water** *(105°–115°F/41°–46°C)*
1 tbsp. plus 3/4 tsp. (10 g) **active dry yeast**
1 tbsp. (15 g) **powdered milk**
1/2 stick (50 g) **unsalted butter**, *softened*
1 tbsp. plus 1 tsp. (25 g) **salt**

Put the flour and milk powder on a clean work surface and make a well in the
center. Dissolve the yeast in the water and pour the yeast mixture into the well.
Gradually start incorporating the yeast mixture into the flour mixture until a loose
dough starts to form, then add the butter and the salt. Knead until
the dough is smooth and elastic.
Heat the oven to 360°F (180°C). Cover the dough with a sheet of plastic wrap
and let it rest for about 10 minutes; then divide it into pieces, each weighing
about 1 1/2 ounces (40 g). Roll the pieces into small balls and arrange them,
floured and well spaced, in a baking pan lined with parchment paper. Let the
dough rise in a warm place, covered with a sheet of plastic wrap, until it has
doubled in size, about 1 hour. Bake for about 20 minutes, or until golden brown.

HONEY ROLLS

Preparation time: 10 minutes   Rising time: 1 hour 10 minutes
Cooking time: 15 minutes   Difficulty: easy

10 SERVINGS

8 cups (1 kg) **all-purpose flour or cake flour**, *plus more as needed*
2 cups (450 ml) **warm water** *(105°–115°F/41°–46°C)*
1 tbsp. plus 3/4 tsp. (10 g) **active dry yeast**
2/3 cup (200 g) **honey**, *plus more as needed*
3 tbsp. (40 g) **unsalted butter**, *softened*
1 tbsp. plus 1 tsp. (25 g) **salt**

Put the flour on a clean work surface and make a well in the center. Dissolve the
yeast in the water and pour the yeast mixture into the well. Gradually start
incorporating the yeast mixture into the flour until a loose dough starts to form,
then add the honey, the butter and the salt. Knead until the dough
is smooth and elastic.

Heat the oven to 350°F (175°C). Cover the dough with a sheet of plastic wrap
and let it rest for about 10 minutes; then make into small balls, each weighing
about 1 3/4 ounces (50 g), using silicone molds if you wish. Arrange the balls in a
baking pan lined with parchment paper. Let the dough rise in a warm place,
covered with a sheet of plastic wrap, until it has doubled in size, about 1 hour. If
desired, drizzle a little honey on the surface of the rolls. Bake for about 15
minutes, or until golden brown.

PARMIGIANO-REGGIANO ROLLS

Preparation time: 10 minutes   Rising time: 1 hour 10 minutes
Cooking time: 15 minutes   Difficulty: easy

10 SERVINGS

8 cups (1 kg) **all-purpose flour or cake flour**, *plus more as needed*
2 1/8 cups (500 ml) **warm milk** *(105°–115°F/41°–46°C)*
1 tbsp. plus 3/4 tsp. (10 g) **active dry yeast**
5 1/4 oz. (150 g) **Parmigiano-Reggiano cheese**, *grated*
3 tbsp. (40 g) **unsalted butter**, *softened*
1 tbsp. plus 1 tsp. (25 g) **salt**

Put the flour and Parmigiano-Reggiano on a clean work surface and make a well in the center. Dissolve the yeast in the milk and pour the yeast mixture into the well. Gradually start incorporating the yeast mixture into the flour until a loose dough starts to form, then add the butter and the salt.
Knead until the dough is smooth and elastic.
Heat the oven to 360°F (180°C). Cover the dough with a sheet of plastic wrap and let it rest for about 10 minutes; then make it into small balls, each weighing about 1 3/4 ounces (50 g). Arrange them, floured and well spaced, in a baking pan lined with parchment paper and let them rise, covered with a sheet of plastic wrap, for about an hour until they have doubled in size. Sprinkle the surface of the rolls with a little Parmigiano-Reggiano cheese. Bake for about 15 minutes, or until golden brown.

GOLDEN-RAISIN ROLLS

Preparation time: 10 minutes   Rising time: 1 hour 10 minutes
Cooking time: 20 minutes   Difficulty: easy

10 SERVINGS

8 cups (1 kg) **all-purpose flour or cake flour**, *plus more as needed*
2 1/8 cups (500 ml) **warm water** *(105°–115°F/41°–46°C)*
1 tbsp. plus 3/4 tsp. (10 g) **active dry yeast**
1 cup (130 g) **golden raisins** *(sultanas)*
3 tbsp. (40 g) **unsalted butter**, *softened*
1 tbsp. plus 1 tsp. (25 g) **salt**

Soak the raisins in water for about 2 hours. Meanwhile, put the flour on a clean work surface and make a well in the center. Dissolve the yeast in the water and pour the yeast mixture into the well. Gradually start incorporating the yeast mixture into the flour until a loose dough starts to form, then add the butter. Pat the golden raisins dry and add them to the mixture. Lastly, add the salt and knead until the dough is smooth and elastic.

Heat the oven to 350°F (175°C). Cover the dough with a sheet of plastic wrap and let it rest for about 10 minutes; then form small balls, each weighing about 1 1/2 ounces (40 g)—or create shapes of your choice. Arrange them, floured and well spaced, in a baking pan lined with parchment paper. Let the dough rise in a warm place, covered with a sheet of plastic wrap, until it has doubled in size, about 1 hour. Bake for about 20 minutes, or until golden brown.

ONION ROLLS

Preparation time: 30 minutes   Rising time: 1 hour 10 minutes
Cooking time: 15 minutes   Difficulty: easy

10 SERVINGS

8 cups (1 kg) **all-purpose flour or cake flour**, *plus more as needed*
1 **red onion**, *preferably Tropea, diced small*
2 1/8 cups (500 ml) **warm water** *(105°–115°F/41°–46°C)*
1 tbsp. plus 3/4 tsp. (10 g) **active dry yeast**
2 3/4 tbsp. (40 ml) **extra-virgin olive oil**
1 tbsp. plus 1 tsp. (25 g) **salt**
Splash of **white wine**, *optional*

Heat the olive oil in a saucepan and sauté the onion lightly. Add white wine, if desired. Continue to cook until the onion is soft and the wine has evaporated, then remove from the heat and let cool. Put the flour on a clean work surface and make a well in the center. Dissolve the yeast in the water and pour the yeast mixture into the well. Gradually start incorporating the yeast mixture into the flour until a loose dough starts to form, then add the sautéed onion and the salt. Knead until the dough is smooth and elastic.

Heat oven to 360°F (180°C). Cover the dough with a sheet of plastic wrap and let rest for about 10 minutes; then make it into small balls, each weighing about 1 3/4 ounces (50 g). Arrange the rolls, floured and well spaced, in a baking pan lined with parchment paper. If desired, garnish each with a few pieces of onion. Let the dough rise in a warm place, covered with a sheet of plastic wrap, until it has doubled in size, about 1 hour. Bake for about 15 minutes, or until golden brown.

OLIVE ROLLS

Preparation time: 10 minutes   Rising time: 1 hour 10 minutes
Cooking time: 12 minutes   Difficulty: easy

10 SERVINGS

8 cups (1 kg) **all-purpose flour or cake flour***, plus more as needed*
2 1/3 cups (550 ml) **warm water** *(105°–115°F/41°–46°C)*
3 1/2 oz. (100 g) **green and black olives***, pitted*
2 3/4 tbsp. (40 ml) **extra-virgin olive oil**
1 tbsp. plus 3/4 tsp. (10 g) **active dry yeast**
1 tbsp. plus 1 tsp. (25 g) **salt**

Chop the olives coarsely, making sure you do not squeeze out the oil. Put the flour on a clean work surface and make a well in the center. Dissolve the yeast in the water and pour the yeast mixture into the well. Gradually start incorporating the yeast mixture into the flour until a loose dough starts to form, then add the oil, the olives and a little flour to absorb the oil from the olives. Lastly, add the salt and continue to knead until the dough is smooth and elastic.

Heat the oven to 350°F (175°C). Cover the dough with a sheet of plastic wrap and let it rest for about 10 minutes; then form small rolls, each weighing about 1 3/4 ounces (50 g). Arrange the rolls, floured and well spaced, in a baking pan lined with parchment paper. Let the dough rise in a warm place, covered with a sheet of plastic wrap, until it has doubled in size, about 1 hour. Bake for about 12 minutes.

PRUNE ROLLS

Preparation time: 10 minutes   Rising time: 1 hour 10 minutes
Cooking time: 20 minutes   Difficulty: easy

10 SERVINGS

8 cups (1 kg) **all-purpose flour or cake flour**, *plus more as needed*
2 1/2 cups (600 ml) **warm water** *(105°–115°F/41°–46°C)*
1 tbsp. plus 3/4 tsp. (10 g) **active dry yeast**
20 **pitted prunes**, *julienned*
3 tbsp. (40 g) **unsalted butter**, *softened*
1 tbsp. plus 1 tsp. (25 g) **salt**

Put the flour on a clean work surface and make a well in the center. Dissolve the yeast in the water and pour the yeast mixture into the well. Gradually start incorporating the yeast mixture into the flour until a loose dough starts to form, then add the butter, the prunes and the salt. Continue to knead until the dough is smooth and elastic.

Heat the oven to 360°F (180°C). Cover the dough with a sheet of plastic wrap and let it rest for about 10 minutes; then form small balls, each weighing about 1 1/2 ounces (40 g)—or create shapes of your choice. Arrange the rolls, floured and well spaced, in a baking pan lined with parchment paper.

Let the dough rise in a warm place, covered with a sheet of plastic wrap, until it has doubled in size, about 1 hour. Bake for about 20 minutes.

YOGURT ROLLS

Preparation time: 10 minutes   Rising time: 1 hour 10 minutes
Cooking time: 15 minutes   Difficulty: medium

10 SERVINGS

8 cups (1 kg) **all-purpose flour or cake flour**, *plus more as needed*
1 1/4 cups (300 ml) **warm milk**
1 cup (250 g) **plain yogurt** *(low- or full-fat)*
3 tbsp. (40 g) **unsalted butter**, *softened*
1 tbsp. plus 3/4 tsp. (10 g) **active dry yeast**
1 tbsp. plus 1 tsp. (25 g) **salt**

Put the flour on a clean work surface and make a well in the center. Dissolve the yeast in the milk and pour the yeast mixture into the well. Gradually start incorporating the yeast mixture into the flour until a loose dough starts to form, then add the yogurt, the butter and the salt. Knead until the dough is smooth and elastic.

Heat the oven to 340°F (170°C). Cover the dough with a sheet of plastic wrap and let it rest for about 10 minutes; then divide it into small pieces, each weighing about 1 1/2 ounces (40 g). Place the pieces of dough in 10 small blancmange molds or ovenproof ramekins. Let the dough rise in a warm place, covered with a sheet of plastic wrap, until it has doubled in size, about 1 hour. Bake for about 15 minutes, or until golden brown.

BREAD TRIANGLES
WITH RADICCHIO DI TREVISO

Preparation time: 10 minutes   Rising time: 1 hour 10 minutes
Cooking time: 20 minutes   Difficulty: easy

10 SERVINGS

8 cups (1 kg) **all-purpose flour or cake flour**, plus more as needed
2 1/8 cups (500 ml) **warm water** (105°–115°F/41°–46°C)
1 tbsp. plus 3/4 tsp. (10 g) **active dry yeast**
3 **heads radicchio**, preferably radicchio di Treviso, finely chopped
3 tbsp. (40 g) **unsalted butter**, softened
1 tbsp. plus 1 tsp. (25 g) **salt**

Put the flour on a clean work surface and make a well in the center. Dissolve the yeast in the water and pour the yeast mixture into the well. Gradually start incorporating the yeast mixture into the flour until a loose dough starts to form, then add the butter, the radicchio, and the salt. Knead until the dough is smooth and elastic.

Heat the oven to 350°F (175°C). Cover the dough with a sheet of plastic and let it rest for about 10 minutes. Then divide it into balls, each weighing about 3 1/2 ounces (100 g), and make them into triangular shapes. Arrange the triangles, floured and well spaced, in a baking pan lined with parchment paper. Let the dough rise in a warm place, covered with a sheet of plastic wrap, until it has doubled in size, about 1 hour. Bake for about 20 minutes, or until golden brown.

RYE TRIANGLES

Preparation time: 10 minutes   Rising time: 1 hour 10 minutes
Cooking time: 12 minutes   Difficulty: easy

10 SERVINGS

4 3/4 cups (600 g) **all-purpose flour or cake flour**, *plus more as needed*
4 cups (400 g) **rye flour**, *plus more as needed*
2 1/2 cups (600 ml) **warm water** *(105°–115°F/41°–46°C)*
2 3/4 tbsp. (40 ml) **extra-virgin olive oil**
4 1/4 tsp. (12 g) **active dry yeast**
1 tbsp. plus 1 tsp. (25 g) **salt**

Combine the two types of flour. Dissolve the yeast in the water and pour the yeast mixture into the well. Gradually start incorporating the yeast mixture into the flour until a loose dough starts to form, then add the olive oil and the salt. Knead until the dough is smooth and elastic.
Heat the oven to 350°F (175°C). Cover the dough with a sheet of plastic wrap and let it rest for about 10 minutes; then form small triangular rolls, each weighing about 1 3/4 ounces (50 g). Arrange them, floured and well spaced, in a baking pan lined with parchment paper. Let the dough rise in a warm place, covered with a sheet of plastic wrap, until it has doubled in size, about 1 hour. Using a sharp knife or a razor blade, make small cuts on the surface of the triangles. Bake for about 12 minutes.

BREADSTICKS AND

Napoleon Bonaparte called them "Turin's little sticks," and he was crazy about them. He had them delivered directly from the capital of Piedmont. According to legend, breadsticks, those crunchy little rods, were invented in 1679 by Antonio Brunero, a baker from Turin, to help cure the stomach ailments of the young Duke Vittorio Amadeo II of Savoy. Legend also has it that the breadsticks were successful. It's more likely that the first breadsticks—whether rolled or formed by hand, and covered with a thin layer of flour—were baked simply to last a long time during periods of famine (their lower moisture content made that possible).

Today, breadsticks are often served with with cold cuts and cheeses or during a wine tasting, and can be enriched with every possible ingredient, from vegetables—such as celery, shallots or spinach—to herbs—like sage, rosemary, basil or marjoram. They may contain little bits of green or black olives, or they may be sprinkled with sesame or poppy seeds. In short, they are so

CRACKERS

delicious on their own, they hardly need an accompaniment.

Even the ancestors of crackers were made in Italy, as far back as the sixteenth century. Sailors' biscuits (or hardtack) were intended to remain fresh for weeks, even months, on a ship's long journey. The type of crackers that we know today—those crispy thin rectangles of tasty dough—were born in Milton, Massachusetts, in the early nineteenth century (again, as sailors' rations).

They were introduced to Italy in 1955, thanks to an entrepreneur from Pavia who understood their potential. And they affirmed themselves immediately, both for the table and as a light snack.

Just like breadsticks, crackers can be flavored with herbs, like oregano or chives, embellished with oilseeds, such as linseed or sunflower seeds, or enhanced with numerous ingredients to make new flavors. They can accompany any dish, but, with their pleasing crispiness, they are excellent completely on their own.

BREADSTICKS
WITH WHEAT GERM

Preparation time: 10 minutes   Rising time: 50 minutes
Cooking time: 15 minutes   Difficulty: medium

10 SERVINGS

8 cups (1 kg) **all-purpose flour or cake flour**, *plus more as needed*
2 1/2 cups (600 ml) **warm water** *(105°–115°F/41°–46°C)*
7 tbsp. (50 g) **wheat germ**, *plus more as needed*
1 1/2 tsp. (4 g) **active dry yeast**
3 tbsp. plus 1 tsp. (50 ml) **extra-virgin olive oil**, *plus more as needed*
1 tbsp. (20 g) **salt**
***Semolina flour**, as needed*

Put the flour and wheat germ on a clean work surface and make a well in the center. Gradually start incorporating the yeast mixture into the flour mixture until a loose dough starts to form, then add the oil and the salt. Knead until the dough is smooth and soft. Brush the dough with oil and let it rest, covered with a sheet of plastic wrap, for about 20 minutes.

Heat the oven to 360°F (180°C). Cut the dough into 2-inch slices and stretch them out into 14-inch-long cylinders, the typical shape of breadsticks. You can also make the breadsticks by rolling them on a cutting board using both hands. If desired, sprinkle with more wheat germ to create a light breading effect. Arrange the breadsticks, well spaced, in a baking pan lined with parchment paper. Sprinkle them with a little semolina and let the dough rise in a warm, humid place, covered with a sheet of plastic wrap, about 30 minutes. Bake for about 15 minutes, or until golden brown and crispy.

CELERY BREADSTICKS

*Preparation time: 15 minutes   Rising time: 50 minutes
Cooking time: 15 minutes   Difficulty: medium*

10 SERVINGS

8 cups (1 kg) **all-purpose flour or cake flour**, plus more as needed
9 stalks (575 g) **celery**
1 1/2 tsp. (4 g) **active dry yeast**
3 tbsp. plus 1 tsp. (50 ml) **extra-virgin olive oil**, plus more as needed
1 tbsp. (20 g) **salt**
Semolina flour, as needed

Prepare the blended celery: wash the celery, remove the outermost stalks and in a blender, blend 6 stalks and the leaves until puréed. Finely chop the remaining 3 celery stalks. Put the flour on a clean work surface and make a well in the center. Dissolve the yeast in the water and pour the yeast mixture into the well. Gradually start incorporating the yeast mixture into the flour mixture until a loose dough starts to form, then add the oil, the blended celery, chopped celery and the salt. Knead until the dough is smooth and soft. Brush the dough with oil and let it rest, covered with a sheet of plastic wrap, for about 20 minutes.
Heat the oven to 360 (180°C). Cut the dough into 2-inch slices and stretch them into 14-inch-long cylinders, the typical shape of breadsticks. You can also make the breadsticks by rolling them on a cutting board using both hands.
Arrange the breadsticks, well spaced, in a baking pan lined with parchment paper. Sprinkle them with a little semolina and let the dough rise in a warm, humid place, covered with a sheet of plastic wrap, about 30 minutes. Bake for about 15 minutes, or until golden brown and crispy.

BARLEY BREADSTICKS

Preparation time: 10 minutes Rising time: 50 minutes
Cooking time: 15 minutes Difficulty: medium

10 SERVINGS

4 3/4 cups (600 g) **all-purpose flour or cake flour**, *plus more as needed*
2 3/4 cups (400 g) **barley flour**
2 1/2 cups (600 ml) **warm water** *(105°–115°F/41°–46°C)*
1 1/2 tsp. (4 g) **active dry yeast**
3 tbsp. plus 1 tsp. (50 ml) **extra-virgin olive oil**, *plus more as needed*
1 tbsp. (20 g) **salt**
Semolina flour, *as needed*

Mix the two types of flour, put them on a clean work surface and make a well in the mixture. Dissolve the yeast in the water and pour the yeast mixture into the well. Gradually start incorporating the yeast mixture into the flour mixture until a loose dough starts to form, then add the oil and the salt. Knead until the dough is smooth and soft. Brush the dough with oil and let it rest, covered with plastic wrap, for about 20 minutes.

Heat the oven to 360°F (180°C). Cut the dough into small slices and stretch them into thin cylinders, the typical shape of breadsticks. You can also make the breadsticks by rolling them on a cutting board using both hands. Arrange the breadsticks, well spaced, in a baking pan lined with parchment paper. Sprinkle them with a little semolina and let the dough rise in a warm, humid place, covered with a sheet of plastic wrap, about 30 minutes. Bake for about 15 minutes, or until golden brown and crispy.

PAPRIKA BREADSTICKS

Preparation time: 10 minutes   Rising time: 50 minutes
Cooking time: 15 minutes   Difficulty: medium

10 SERVINGS

8 cups (1 kg) **all-purpose flour or cake flour**, *plus more as needed*
2 1/2 cups (600 ml) **warm water** *(105°–115°F/41°–46°C)*
1 heaping tbsp. (8 g) **paprika**
1 1/2 tsp. (4 g) **active dry yeast**
3 tbsp. plus 1 tsp. (50 ml) **extra-virgin olive oil**, *plus more as needed*
1 tbsp. (20 g) **salt**
Semolina flour, *as needed*

Put the flour and paprika on a clean work surface and make a well in the center.
Dissolve the yeast in the water and pour the yeast mixture into the well.
Gradually start incorporating the yeast mixture into the flour mixture until a loose
dough starts to form, then add the oil and the salt. Knead until the dough is
smooth and soft. Brush the dough with oil and let it rest, covered with a sheet of
plastic wrap, for about 20 minutes.
Heat the oven to 360°F (180°C). Cut the dough into small slices and stretch them
into thin cylinders, the typical shape of breadsticks. You can also make the
breadsticks by rolling them on a cutting board using both hands. Arrange the
breadsticks, well spaced, in a baking pan lined with parchment paper. Sprinkle
them with a little semolina and let the dough rise in a warm, humid place,
covered with a sheet of plastic wrap, about 30 minutes. Bake for about 15
minutes, or until golden brown and crispy.

SAGE BREADSTICKS

Preparation time: 10 minutes   Rising time: 50 minutes
Cooking time: 15 minutes   Difficulty: medium

10 SERVINGS

8 cups (1 kg) **all-purpose flour or cake flour**, plus more as needed
2 1/2 cups (600 ml) **warm water** (105°–115°F/41°–46°C)
15 **fresh sage leaves**
1 1/2 tsp. (4 g) **active dry yeast**
3 tbsp. plus 1 tsp. (50 ml) **extra-virgin olive oil**, plus more as needed
1 tbsp. (20 g) **salt**
Semolina flour, as needed

Rinse and dry the sage leaves. Tear them into tiny pieces and add them to the
oil. Put the flour on a clean work surface and make a well in the center. Dissolve
the yeast in the water and pour the yeast mixture into the well. Gradually start
incorporating the yeast mixture into the flour until a loose dough starts to form,
then add the oil with sage and the salt. Knead until the dough is smooth and
soft. Brush the dough with oil and let it rest, covered with a sheet of plastic wrap,
for about 20 minutes.
Heat the oven to 360°F (180°C). Cut the dough into small slices and stretch them
into thin cylinders, the typical shape of breadsticks. You can also make the
breadsticks by rolling them on a cutting board using both hands. Arrange the
breadsticks, well spaced, in a baking pan lined with parchment paper. Sprinkle
them with a little semolina and let the dough rise in a warm, humid place,
covered with a sheet of plastic wrap, about 30 minutes. Bake for about 15
minutes, or until golden brown and crispy.

WHOLE-WHEAT BREADSTICKS

Preparation time: 10 minutes Rising time: 50 minutes
Cooking time: 15 minutes Difficulty: medium

10 SERVINGS

4 cups (500 g) **all-purpose flour or cake flour**, *plus more as needed*
4 cups (500 g) **whole-wheat flour**
2 3/4 cups (650 ml) **warm water** *(105°–115°F/41°–46°C)*
2 1/4 tsp. (6 g) **active dry yeast**
3 tbsp. plus 1 tsp. (50 ml) **extra-virgin olive oil**, *plus more as needed*
1 tbsp. (20 g) **salt**
Semolina flour, *as needed*

Combine the flours. Put the flours on a clean work surface and make a well in the center. Dissolve the yeast in the water and pour the yeast mixture into the well. Gradually start incorporating the yeast mixture into the flour mixture until a loose dough starts to form, then add the oil and the salt. Knead until the dough is smooth and soft. Brush the dough with oil and let it rest, covered with a sheet of plastic wrap, for about 20 minutes.

Heat the oven to 360°F (180°C). Cut the dough into small slices and stretch them into thin cylinders, the typical shape of breadsticks. You can also make the breadsticks by rolling them on a cutting board using both hands. Arrange the breadsticks, well spaced, in a baking pan lined with parchment paper. Sprinkle them with a little semolina and let the dough rise in a warm, humid place, covered with a sheet of plastic wrap, about 30 minutes. Bake for about 15 minutes, or until golden brown and crispy.

HERB FLATBREAD

Preparation time: 20 minutes   Rising time: 1 hour
Cooking time: 12 minutes   Difficulty: medium

4 SERVINGS

4 cups (500 g) **all-purpose flour or cake flour**
1 cup (250 ml) **warm milk**
1 1/4 tsp. (3 g) **active dry yeast**
2/3 tsp. (5 g) **malt** or 1 1/4 tsp. (5 g) **sugar**
1 tbsp. plus 2 tsp. (25 ml) **extra-virgin olive oil,** *plus more as needed*
1 **bunch of fresh herbs** *(sage, rosemary, thyme), chopped*
1 tsp. (7 g) **salt**
Water, *as needed*

On a clean surface, mix the flour with the malt or sugar and the herbs. Add the yeast and gradually add the milk, and begin to knead. Then add the oil and the salt, and continue to knead until the dough is smooth and elastic. If it is too firm, soften it with a little warm water. Let the dough rise in a warm place, covered with a sheet of plastic wrap, until it has doubled in size, about 1 hour.

Heat the oven to 360°F (180°C). Roll out the dough with a rolling pin to a thickness of 1/12 inch (2 mm), cut it into shapes of your choice and place them on a baking sheet greased with olive oil. Prick the dough with a fork to keep the flatbread from puffing up during baking. Bake for about 12 minutes, or until golden brown and crispy.

MANTUA FLATBREAD

Preparation time: 15 minutes   Rising time: 3 hours 20 minutes
Cooking time: 20 minutes   Difficulty: medium

4 SERVINGS

4 cups (500 g) **all-purpose flour or cake flour**
1 cup plus 2 1/2 tbsp. (275 ml) **warm water** *(105°–115°F/41°–46°C)*
2 1/4 tsp. (6 g) **active dry yeast**
1 1/4 tsp. (5 g) **sugar**
5 tbsp. (75 ml) **extra-virgin olive oil**, *plus more as needed*
2 1/2 tsp. (15 g) **salt**

On a clean surface, mix the flour and the sugar. Add the yeast and begin to knead, gradually adding the water. Then add the olive oil and the salt, and continue to knead until the dough is smooth and elastic. Let the dough rise in a warm place, covered with a sheet of plastic wrap, until it has doubled in size, about 1 hour. Heat the oven to 360°F (180°C). Divide the dough into pieces of about 2 ounces (60 grams) each. Place them, well spaced, on a baking sheet greased with oil and let them rest for about 20 minutes. Flatten them with your hands and let them rise for about 2 hours. Bake for about 20 minutes.

TARALLI

Preparation time: 1 hour   Cooking time: 30 minutes   Difficulty: medium

10 SERVINGS

4 cups (500 g) **all-purpose flour or cake flour**
1/2 cup (100 ml) **dry white wine**
1/2 cup (120 ml) **extra-virgin olive oil**, *plus more as needed*
1 2/3 tsp. (10 g) **salt**
Warm water *(105°–115°F/41°–46°C), as needed*

On a clean surface, mix the flour with the white wine, olive oil, salt and enough water to obtain a smooth and elastic dough. Cover the dough in a sheet of plastic wrap and let it rest for at least 15 minutes, then divide the dough into ropes about 1/3 inch (1 cm) in diameter. Cut them into pieces about 3 inches (8 cm) long and make them into small rings by joining the two ends of the dough. Heat the oven to 350°F (175°C). Drop the rings into a pot of salted boiling water. When they rise to the surface, use a slotted spoon to transfer them to a kitchen towel to dry. Line them up on a lightly oiled baking pan. Bake for about 30 minutes, or until golden brown.

HERB CRACKERS

Preparation time: 10 minutes   Rising time: 50 minutes
Cooking time: 15 minutes   Difficulty: easy

10 SERVINGS

8 cups (1 kg) **all-purpose flour or cake flour**
2 1/3 cups (550 ml) **warm water** *(105°–115°F/41°–46°C)*
6 tbsp. plus 2 tsp. (40 g) **chopped fresh herbs**
(such as rosemary, chives, bay leaves, oregano, marjoram, sage)
1 tbsp. (8 g) **active dry yeast**
3 tbsp. plus 1 tsp. (50 ml) **extra-virgin olive oil**, *plus more as needed*
1 tbsp. (20 g) **salt**

Put a mix of chopped herbs and spices in the olive oil. Put the flour on a clean work surface and make a well in the center. Dissolve the yeast in the water and pour the yeast mixture into the well. Gradually start incorporating the yeast mixture into the flour mixture until a loose dough starts to form, then add the oil with herbs and spices and the salt. Knead until the dough is smooth and soft. Let the dough rest, covered with a sheet of plastic wrap, for about 10 minutes. Heat the oven to 360°F (180°C). Roll out the dough with a rolling pin to a thickness of about 1/25 inch (1 mm). Cut into pieces with a fluted pastry wheel and arrange in a baking pan lined with parchment paper. Let the dough rise in a warm, humid place, covered with a sheet of plastic wrap, about 40 minutes. Prick the dough with a fork to keep the crackers from puffing up during baking. Bake for about 15 minutes, or until golden and crispy.

LIME CRACKERS

Preparation time: 10 minutes   Rising time: 50 minutes
Cooking time: 15 minutes   Difficulty: easy

10 SERVINGS

8 cups (1 kg) **all-purpose flour or cake flour**
2 1/3 cups (550 ml) **warm water** *(105°–115°F/41°–46°C)*
Zest of 2 **limes**
1 tbsp. (8 g) **active dry yeast**
3 tbsp. plus 1 tsp. (50 ml) **extra-virgin olive oil,** *plus more as needed*
1 tbsp. (20 g) **salt**

Put the lime zest in the olive oil. Put the flour on a clean work surface and make
a well in the center. Dissolve the yeast in the water and pour the yeast mixture
into the well. Gradually start incorporating the yeast mixture into the flour
mixture until a loose dough starts to form, then add the oil with the lime zest
and the salt. Knead until the dough is smooth and soft. Let the dough rest,
covered with a sheet of plastic wrap, for about 10 minutes.
Heat the oven to 360°F (180°C). Roll out the dough with a rolling pin to a
thickness of about 1/25 inch (1 mm). Cut into pieces with a fluted pastry wheel
and arrange in a baking pan lined with parchment paper. Let the dough rise in a
warm, humid place, covered with a sheet of plastic wrap, about 40 minutes. Prick
the dough with a fork to keep the crackers from puffing up during baking. Bake
for about 15 minutes, or until golden and crispy.

ROSEMARY CRACKERS

Preparation time: 10 minutes   Rising time: 50 minutes
Cooking time: 15 minutes   Difficulty: easy

10 SERVINGS

8 cups (1 kg) **all-purpose flour or cake flour**
2 1/3 cups (550 ml) **warm water (105°–115°F/41°–46°C)**
4 **sprigs of rosemary**
1 tbsp. (8 g) **active dry yeast**
3 tbsp. plus 1 tsp. (50 ml) **extra-virgin olive oil**
1 tbsp. (20 g) **salt**

Put the rosemary needles in the olive oil. Put the flour on a clean work surface and make a well in the center. Dissolve the yeast in the water and pour the yeast mixture into the well. Gradually start incorporating the yeast mixture into the flour mixture until a loose dough starts to form, then add the oil with the rosemary and the salt. Knead until the dough is smooth and soft. Let the dough rest, covered with a sheet of plastic wrap, for about 10 minutes.

Heat the oven to 360°F (180°C). Roll out the dough with a rolling pin to a thickness of about 1/25 inch (1 mm). Cut into pieces with a fluted pastry wheel and arrange in a baking pan lined with parchment paper. Let the dough rise in a warm, humid place, covered with a sheet of plastic wrap, about 40 minutes. Prick the dough with a fork to keep the crackers from puffing up during baking. Bake for about 15 minutes, or until golden brown and crispy.

GARLIC CRACKERS

Preparation time: 10 minutes   Rising time: 50 minutes
Cooking time: 15 minutes   Difficulty: easy

10 SERVINGS

8 cups (1 kg) **all-purpose flour or cake flour**
2 1/3 cups (550 ml) **warm water** (105°–115°F/41°–46°C)
1 clove **garlic**, minced
1 tbsp. (8 g) **active dry yeast**
3 tbsp. plus 1 tsp. (50 ml) **extra-virgin olive oil**
1 tbsp. (20 g) **salt**

Put the garlic in the olive oil. Put the flour on a clean work surface and make a well in the center. Dissolve the yeast in the water and pour the yeast mixture into the well. Gradually start incorporating the yeast mixture into the flour mixture until a loose dough starts to form, then add the oil with the garlic and the salt. Knead until the dough is smooth and soft. Let the dough rest, covered with a sheet of plastic wrap, for about 10 minutes.

Heat the oven to 360°F (180°C). Roll out the dough with a rolling pin to a thickness of about 1/25 inch (1 mm). Cut into pieces with a fluted pastry wheel and arrange in a baking pan lined with parchment paper. Let the dough rise in a warm, humid place, covered with a sheet of plastic wrap, about 40 minutes. Prick the dough with a fork to keep the crackers from puffing up during baking. Bake for about 15 minutes, or until golden and crispy.

CHIVE CRACKERS

Preparation time: 10 minutes   Rising time: 50 minutes
Cooking time: 15 minutes   Difficulty: easy

10 SERVINGS

8 cups (1 kg) **all-purpose flour or cake flour**
2 1/3 cups (550 ml) **warm water** *(105°–115°F/41°–46°C)*
1 small bunch of **fresh chives***, snipped*
1 tbsp. (8 g) **active dry yeast**
3 tbsp. plus 1 tsp. (50 ml) **extra-virgin olive oil**
1 tbsp. (20 g) **salt**

Put the chives in the olive oil. Put the flour on a clean work surface and make a well in the center. Dissolve the yeast in the water and pour the yeast mixture into the well. Gradually start incorporating the yeast mixture into the flour mixture until a loose dough starts to form, then add the oil with the chives and the salt. Knead until the dough is smooth and soft. Let the dough rest, covered with a sheet of plastic wrap, for about 10 minutes.

Heat the oven to 360°F (180°C). Roll out the dough with a rolling pin to a thickness of about 1/25 inch (1 mm). Cut into pieces with a fluted pastry wheel and arrange in a baking pan lined with parchment paper. Let the dough rise in a warm, humid place, covered with a sheet of plastic wrap, about 40 minutes. Prick the dough with a fork to keep the crackers from puffing up during baking. Bake for about 15 minutes, or until lightly golden and crispy.

OREGANO CRACKERS

Preparation time: 10 minutes   Rising time: 50 minutes
Cooking time: 15 minutes   Difficulty: easy

10 SERVINGS

8 cups (1 kg) **all-purpose flour or cake flour**
2 1/3 cups (550 ml) **warm water** *(105°–115°F/41°–46°C)*
1 tbsp. (5 g) **dried or fresh oregano**
1 tbsp. (8 g) **active dry yeast**
3 tbsp. plus 1 tsp. (50 ml) **extra-virgin olive oil**
1 tbsp. (20 g) **salt**

Put the oregano in the olive oil. Put the flour on a clean work surface and make a well in the center. Dissolve the yeast in the water and pour the yeast mixture into the well. Gradually start incorporating the yeast mixture into the flour mixture until a loose dough starts to form, then add the oil with the oregano and the salt. Knead until the dough is šmooth and soft. Let the dough rest, covered with a sheet of plastic wrap, for about 10 minutes.

Heat the oven to 360°F (180°C). Roll out the dough with a rolling pin to a thickness of about 1/25 inch (1 mm). Cut into pieces with a fluted pastry wheel and arrange in a baking pan lined with parchment paper. Let the dough rise in a warm, humid place, covered with a sheet of plastic wrap, about 40 minutes. Prick the dough with a fork to keep the crackers from puffing up during baking. Bake for about 15 minutes, or until golden brown and crispy.

GINGER CRACKERS

Preparation time: 10 minutes   Rising time: 50 minutes
Cooking time: 15 minutes   Difficulty: easy

10 SERVINGS

8 cups (1 kg) all-purpose flour or cake flour
2 1/3 cups (550 ml) warm water (105°–115°F/41°–46°C)
3/4 oz. (20 g) fresh ginger, peeled and thinly sliced
1 tbsp. (8 g) active dry yeast
3 tbsp. plus 1 tsp. (50 ml) extra-virgin olive oil
1 tbsp. (20 g) salt

Put the ginger in the olive oil. Put the flour on a clean work surface and make a well in the center. Dissolve the yeast in the water and pour the yeast mixture into the well. Gradually start incorporating the yeast mixture into the flour mixture until a loose dough starts to form, then add the oil with the ginger and the salt. Knead until the dough is smooth and soft. Let the dough rest, covered with a sheet of plastic wrap, for about 10 minutes.

Heat the oven to 360°F (180°C). Roll out the dough with a rolling pin to a thickness of about 1/25 inch (1 mm). Cut into pieces with a fluted pastry wheel and arrange in a baking pan lined with parchment paper.

Let the dough rise in a warm, humid place, covered with a sheet of plastic wrap, about 40 minutes. Prick the dough with a fork to keep the crackers from puffing up during baking. Bake for about 15 minutes, or until golden brown and crispy.

INGREDIENTS INDEX

PHOTO CREDITS

All photographs are by ACADEMIA BARILLA except the following:
pages 6, 95 ©123RF

. . . .

Original edition © 2013 by De Agostini Libri S.p.A.

The Taunton Press, Inc.
63 South Main Street
PO Box 5506, Newtown, CT 06470-5506
e-mail: tp@taunton.com

Translations:
Catherine Howard - Mary Doyle - John Venerella - Free z'be, Paris
Salvatore Ciolfi - Rosetta Translations SARL - Rosetta Translations SARL

LIBRARY OF CONGRESS CATALOGING-IN-PUBLICATION DATA IN PROGRESS
ISBN: 978-1-62710-052-6

Printed in China
10 9 8 7 6 5 4 3 2 1